REVELATIONS FROM THE VINEYARD OF NABOTH

"The LORD executes righteousness and justice for all who are oppressed."

Psalm 103:6

BOBBY CONNER

THE JUSTICE OF GOD: *Revelations from the Vineyard of Naboth*
Copyright © by Bobby Conner 2009

All rights reserved. No part of this book may be reproduced or transmitted in any form or by any means, electronic, mechanical, including photocopying, recording, or by any information storage and retrieval system, without written permission from the author.

Distributed by Eagles View Ministries
P.O. Box 933
Bullard, Texas 75757 USA

All scripture quotations, unless otherwise indicated, are taken from the New King James Version®. Copyright © 1982 by Thomas Nelson, Inc. Used by permission. All rights reserved.

ISBN: 978-0-98016-396-4

Cover Design & Book Layout: Dustin Bocks

Printed in the United States of America.

CONTENTS

INTRODUCTION
The Straight Paths of Justice—*The Law of Sowing and Reaping* — 5

PART ONE
The Treasure of Naboth's Vineyard—*The Pattern of God's Justice* — 9
Naboth—*The Fruitful, Priestly Man, The Defender of the Inheritance* — 17
Ahab—*The Wicked, Controlled Man, The Pouting Potentate* — 21
Jezebel—*The Wicked, Controlling Woman,*
The Personification of Perversity — 27
Elijah—*The Holy, Humble Prophet, The Voice of Righteousness* — 31

PART TWO
The Rights To Naboth's Vineyard—*The Battle for God's Justice* — 35
The Lying Letter—*Justice Perverted, Righteousness Mocked* — 41
The Death of Naboth—*The Wheels of Justice Begin to Turn* — 45
The Loss of the Vineyard—*Justice Promised, Hope Assured* — 49
The Alarming Appearance—*The Word of Justice Arrives* — 53

PART THREE
Redeeming Naboth's Vineyard — 57
Falling into the Hands of the Living God—*Payday Will Come!* — 59
Justice…the Law of Love—*The Fulfillment of the Word of God* — 69

CONCLUSION
The Way of Love—*Overcoming by the Blood of the Lamb* — 77

INTRODUCTION
The Straight Paths of Justice
UNDERSTANDING THE LAW OF SOWING AND REAPING

More than 38 years ago, my wife and I were invited to attend a meeting that would forever open my eyes to the nature of God's justice.

I was a young preacher in East Texas, just beginning my ministry and hungry for God. That night, my heart was burning for more of the Lord…but I was disappointed when the guest preacher took the floor. The speaker, Dr. R. G. Lee, was quite old, his white suit and white hair a perfect match. As he shuffled to the platform, I impatiently asked my wife Carolyn if we could go. "I don't want to waste my time," I said, "listening to this old man ramble!" My sweet wife quietly asked if we could stay. Not wanting to cause a commotion, I agreed, reluctantly. Little did I know that Carolyn had just given me some of the best advice I had ever received. God Himself was setting me up—and the shock He had in store for me was immense.

After the worship songs ended, the host pastor introduced Dr. Lee. We all responded with subdued applause. I nudged my wife as if to say, "I told you so!" Despite myself, however, I was stunned by Dr. Lee's appearance. With the spotlight shining on his snowy hair and suit, he looked like an angel.

In the most humble voice, he began: "Let us pray." The instant he opened his mouth, welcoming the Spirit of God and releasing anointing for the service, the room filled with electrifying power. His words began to engrave a message on my heart, one that endures to this day.

He had titled his message "Payday, Someday!" I was absolutely captivated. To this day, I have never heard words paint such a vivid portrait. With every Scripture and revelation, the Spirit of God grew stronger and more powerful in my spirit. Brother Lee's words literally came alive in my heart, translating me from the pew and transporting me out of the church building and across time and space into a most extraordinary scene—*the field of Naboth's vineyard* (1 Kings 21).

At the end of message, I approached Dr. Lee to express my appreciation for how God had used him and his inspired words. As he took my hand, he asked for my Bible. Opening the front cover, he wrote, "O magnify the Lord with me, and let us exalt His name together. Psalms 34:1–3," and signed his name. He then placed his hand on my shoulder and prayed that this verse would be a cornerstone for my ministry.

Although this event took place more than three decades ago, his message still burns within my spirit. As this prince of preachers released God's revelation that night in East Texas, the eyes of my heart were opened to the marvelous fact that we have a faithful, loving Father who will always bring about His divine justice. Know in your heart that it is God Who will have the last word.

The Straight Paths of Justice

The LORD executes righteousness and justice for all who are oppressed.

—Psalm 103:6

Behold, the days come, saith the LORD,
that I will raise unto David a righteous Branch,
and a King shall reign and prosper,
and shall execute judgment and justice in the earth.

—Jeremiah 23:5

Of the increase of his government and peace there shall be no end, upon the throne of David, and upon his kingdom, to order it, and to establish with judgment and with justice from henceforth even for ever. The zeal of the LORD of hosts will perform this.

—Isaiah 9:7

PART ONE
Naboth's Vineyard
THE PATTERN OF GOD'S JUSTICE

Almighty God is a God of justice. The Hebrew word for "justice" is *tsedeq*. *Tsedeq*, in fact, is translated not only as "justice" but also, more commonly, as "righteousness," depending on the Scripture's context. These two translations come from the identical Hebrew word, suggesting that God's righteousness *is* His justice.

This identity of righteousness and justice has profound implications for our lives: in order to walk in peace and joy, we must grasp that the ways of God are always righteous *and* always just. If we were to translate those Scriptures citing *tsedeq* using the term justice instead of the more commonly used translation *righteousness*, we would better grasp the far-reaching scope and power of the Lord's justice in our lives:

> The work of **justice** will be peace, and the effect of **justice**, quietness and assurance forever.
> —Isaiah 32:17

> The LORD is exalted, for He dwells on high; He has filled Zion with judgment and **justice**.
>
> (Isaiah 33:5)

> "No weapon formed against you shall prosper, and every tongue which rises against you in judgment You shall condemn. This is the heritage of the servants of the LORD, and their **justice** is from Me," says the LORD.
>
> (Isaiah 54:17)

The Hebrew *tsedeq* derives from a primitive root meaning *straight*, as in a *physically straight way* or *path*. *Tsedeq* suggests a straight path one walks physically or spiritually, as in "paths of righteousness" (Psalm 23:3) or the "path of the just" (Proverbs 4:18).

The word *justice* not only speaks of walking a straight path, but of God's *making* it straight through His fairness and vindication. Never doubt that God always *does* right and *makes* right—His ways and actions are always righteous, just and appropriate. He knows what is best and always works to accomplish His just and righteous will (Romans 8:28). His ways are higher than ours.

God is just as well as *omnipresent*. He knows all and sees all. God is in every place at all times, so He is fully aware of the ways of the just and the unjust. Nothing and no one can escape His knowing: "The Lord is good, a stronghold in the day of trouble; and He *knows them* that trust in Him" (Nahum 1:7). By no means do righteous intentions and deeds—or the plots and tactics of the wicked—go unnoticed. God is always aware of the motives and plans of man.

Because God knows all and is altogether just, His justice occurs in every situation. How does He enact His justice? Through the law of sowing and reaping—planting a seed and gathering a harvest born from that seed—a spiritual principle always in effect.

Spiritual laws and natural laws apply in all circumstances, no matter what a person may sow: sow righteousness, reap righteousness. Sow to the flesh, reap corruption. The very harvest we sow we shall reap, *without question*. Be not deceived—God is not mocked.

Moreover, the harvest of that reaping is always greater than the seed sown: what we give will be returned "running over" (Luke 6:38). If we sow precious, Godly seed, we will reap bountiful sheaves of blessings (Psalm 126:6). If we sow tears, we will reap joy (Psalm 126:5). If we sow *justice*, we will reap great mercy (Hosea 10:12).

If we sow sin, however—if we sow to the wind (the Hebrew word here suggesting vain words or desires)—we will reap the whirlwind (Hosea 8:7). It is significant that the Hebrew word for "whirlwind" (סופה or *cuwphah*) also means *Red Sea*, or the place where the enemies of Israel received *Divine Justice*. If we sow vanity, we *will* reap destruction.

The riveting history of Naboth's vineyard (I Kings 21:1–29) reveals the profound truth and manner of God's justice. I pray that the Spirit of God speaks clearly to your heart as you read this life-changing drama. Take time let yourself experience the sights and sounds of Naboth's vineyard: imagine that you are with him among the vines, standing in the shade of a huge olive tree, observing all that is taking place.

> And it came to pass after these things that Naboth the Jezreelite had a vineyard which was in Jezreel, next to the palace of Ahab king of Samaria.
> So Ahab spoke to Naboth, saying, "Give me your vineyard, that I may have it for a vegetable garden, because it is near, next to my house; and for it I will give you a vineyard better than it. Or, if it seems good to you, I will give you its worth in money." But Naboth

The Justice of God

said to Ahab, "The Lord forbid that I should give the inheritance of my fathers to you!" So Ahab went into his house sullen and displeased because of the word which Naboth the Jezreelite had spoken to him; for he had said, "I will not give you the inheritance of my fathers." And he lay down on his bed, and turned away his face, and would eat no food. But Jezebel his wife came to him, and said to him, "Why is your spirit so sullen that you eat no food?"

He said to her, "Because I spoke to Naboth the Jezreelite, and said to him, 'Give me your vineyard for money; or else, if it pleases you, I will give you another vineyard for it.' And he answered, 'I will not give you my vineyard.'"

Then Jezebel his wife said to him, "You now exercise authority over Israel! Arise, eat food, and let your heart be cheerful; I will give you the vineyard of Naboth the Jezreelite."

And she wrote letters in Ahab's name, sealed them with his seal, and sent the letters to the elders and the nobles who were dwelling in the city with Naboth. She wrote in the letters, saying,

Proclaim a fast, and seat Naboth with high honor among the people; and seat two men, scoundrels, before him to bear witness against him, saying, You have blasphemed God and the king. Then take him out, and stone him, that he may die.

So the men of his city, the elders and nobles who were inhabitants of his city, did as Jezebel had sent to them, as it was written in the letters which she had sent to them. They proclaimed a fast, and seated Naboth with high honor among the people. And two men, scoundrels, came in and sat before him; and the scoundrels witnessed against him, against Naboth, in the presence of the people, saying, "Naboth has blasphemed God and the king!" Then they took him outside the city and stoned him with stones, so that he died. Then they sent to Jezebel, saying, "Naboth has been stoned and is dead."

And it came to pass, when Jezebel heard that Naboth had been stoned and was dead, that Jezebel said to Ahab, "Arise, take possession of the vineyard of Naboth the Jezreelite, which he refused to give you for money; for Naboth is not alive, but dead." So it was, when Ahab heard that Naboth was dead, that Ahab got up and went down to take possession of the vineyard of Naboth the Jezreelite.

Then the word of the Lord came to Elijah the Tishbite, saying,

"Arise, go down to meet Ahab king of Israel, who lives in Samaria. There he is, in the vineyard of Naboth, where he has gone down to take possession of it. You shall speak to him, saying, 'Thus says the Lord: "Have you murdered and also taken possession?"' And you shall speak to him, saying, 'Thus says the Lord: "In the place where dogs licked the blood of Naboth, dogs shall lick your blood, even yours."'"

So Ahab said to Elijah, "Have you found me, O my enemy?"

And he answered, "I have found you, because you have sold yourself to do evil in the sight of the Lord: 'Behold, I will bring calamity on you. I will take away your posterity, and will cut off from Ahab every male in Israel, both bond and free. I will make your house like the house of Jeroboam the son of Nebat, and like the house of Baasha the son of Ahijah, because of the provocation with which you have provoked Me to anger, and made Israel sin.'

And concerning Jezebel the Lord also spoke, saying, 'The dogs shall eat Jezebel by the wall of Jezreel.' The dogs shall eat whoever belongs to Ahab and dies in the city, and the birds of the air shall eat whoever dies in the field."

But there was no one like Ahab who sold himself to do wickedness in the sight of the Lord, because Jezebel his wife stirred him up. And he behaved very abominably in following idols, according to all that the Amorites had done, whom the Lord had cast out before the children of Israel.

So it was, when Ahab heard those words, that he tore his clothes and put sackcloth on his body, and fasted and lay in sackcloth, and went about mourning.

And the word of the Lord came to Elijah the Tishbite, saying, "See how Ahab has humbled himself before Me? Because he has humbled himself before Me, I will not bring the calamity in his days. In the days of his son I will bring the calamity on his house."

Within these passages of Holy Scripture, an account of great greed and unbridled lust unfolds with deadly, devastating results.

At first, the innocent would seem to be overrun by the powerful and wicked, despite the fact that God promises never to permit the righteous to be forsaken (Psalm 37:25): Naboth is brutally murdered. His inheritance is stolen. A great injustice has been served.

Because God is omniscient and omnipresent, however, we are all exposed to His all-seeing eye: "Nothing in all creation can hide from him. Everything is naked and exposed before his eyes"

Naboth's Vineyard

(Hebrews 4:13, NLT). The wicked king Ahab has his plans, but God has His own plans: He responds by sending His prophetic messenger to confront Ahab with a bold warning.

Notice God's clear words of direction to His prophetic vessel: the prophet was told go to a specific place and speak specific words. This act of declaring the Word of the Lord is not reserved for Old Testament prophets: God is still asking His true prophets to confront carnality and rebuke sin at the highest levels of government, culture and society. We, too, must have steadfast, bold prophets willing to stand for justice and righteousness, willing *to go* to specific places and *speak* specific words. The time has come for true prophets of God to confront the wickedness of our land.

But God's prophets are not the only ones called to speak: as the Body of Christ—a just nation of holy priests (I Peter 2:5)—we are all called to take a bold stand against sin. God is asking every believer to cry out for *tsedeq*, justice and righteousness, to pray that the Lord brings forth His Kingdom. God is calling forth the Body of Christ as a *Zadok priesthood* to teach and declare the vast difference between what is holy and what is profane, the clean and unclean (Ezekiel 44:23). It is vital to note that the same Hebrew root for justice and righteousness, *tsedeq*, is also at the root of *Zadok*—צדוק or *tsadowq*. The name *Zadok* literally means "righteous" or "just." When the righteous cry—when the *tsaddiyq* or צדוק cry—God hears and responds. As followers of Christ, we are called to be a city of priests set high upon a hill, shining forth the light of God's love and mercy to a hurting, desperate world.

By considering the main characters in the story of Naboth's garden, we can discover much of what motivates humanity—and what moves God in His justice. In Part One, we will meet the humble and faithful, the rich and powerful, the wicked and wayward. In Part Two, we will explore what it means to battle for our inheritance...and how God's supreme law of Love is always wholly fulfilled through His divine justice in our lives. In Part Three, we will consider the highest principle of divine justice, the law of Love, demonstrated in the Blood of Christ.

We must trust the faithfulness of the Lord: although the wheels of God's justice may turn slowly, they are indeed turning. We must remain steadfast in faith, absolutely confident that God's promises are altogether true. We are never out of His care. His eyes are always upon His children. In short, we must rest upon the promise that *God is good* (Nahum 1:7).

I pray that this study uncovers the surface veneer of our heart's intentions, allowing us to behold the true motives of our soul. Above all, I pray that you may behold and rest in the faithfulness of our Heavenly Father and His loving desire to protect and provide for His children (Psalm 27). You must never forget that, no matter what trials you face, you are never alone. God *is* a God of righteous justice—and He is standing with you.

Naboth

THE FRUITFUL, PRIESTLY MAN
THE DEFENDER OF THE INHERITANCE

This devout man Naboth, a Jew, lived in Jezreel. He was a just, upright man, genuine and hard-working. Today he'd be described as "salt of the earth."

Naboth owned a vineyard—a man *bearing fruit*. The Hebrew name Naboth, נבות or *nabowth*, in fact, literally means *fruit*. This fruitful man loved his God and his family, as well as the small vineyard he owned, close to wicked King Ahab's glorious summer palace. This vineyard had been given to Naboth as a cherished inheritance and was, no doubt, dear to his heart.

In I Kings 21:3, we read just how dear this vineyard was to Naboth. When King Ahab offered to purchase the property, this man of God adamantly refused to part it. Why? The vineyard was his *inheritance from his fathers*: "The LORD forbid that I should give the inheritance of my fathers to you!" The Hebrew term Naboth uses here is "forbid" (חללה or *chaliylah*), *an exclamation of abhorrence*. Ahab's request for Naboth's vineyard was *abhorrent* to this heir to the vineyard. Naboth was passionate about guarding what was rightfully his and refused to trade it for profit, no matter the price. Naboth would not adulterate the uprightness of his heart: he would not trade heavenly principles for swift, earthly gain.

Strikingly, the Hebrew word here translated "forbid"—this *abhorrence*—is also translated as *"flute"*—both linked by the literal and figurative gesture of "being pierced." Flutes are pierced to create the windpipe; abhorrence, one might say, is *a piercing of the soul*—a keen description of the experience of injustice. Naboth was *pierced* with the injustice of Ahab's request for his vineyard. Why was Naboth so pierced by Ahab's offer? The word "inheritance" (נחלה or *nachalah*) used in this passage literally means *to possess* as wealth or *glory*. Ahab had not merely asked to purchase a tract of real estate; he had asked to buy Naboth's covenantal inheritance.

Closely related to the name Naboth is נבא or *naba'*, meaning *bubbling over* or *boiling forth* like steam from a teapot, a term also used to describe the "bubbling-with-speech" prophets of the Old Testament. For years I edited a prophetic journal, *Naba Word*, referring to these prophets of the Old Testament, from whose mouths "bubbled over" the Word of the Lord. The name *Naboth*, then, also suggests a man who was a type of *naba prophet*.

It is no coincidence that Naboth also shares a Hebrew root with נב or *Nob*, which literally means a "high place," and an actual city of priests near Jerusalem. At Nob, David asked the priest Ahimelech for the shewbread to eat with his men. This very city is also where Saul commanded Doeg the Edomite, Saul's chief shepherd, to slay Ahimelech and the priests serving with him (I Sam. 22:18). Note that *Ahimelech*, אחימלך, literally means "brother to the King" and *Doeg*, or דאג , means "fearful."

Also notice here the correlation between the *unjust slaying* of this innocent "brother to the King" and the priests of Nob and the *unjust slaying* of innocent Naboth. Naboth was murdered by order of an evil Queen—her orders carried out by two "sons of Belial" (בליעל or *běliya`al* literally meaning *no fruit*, or *worthless*). These fruitless sons murdered the fruitful heir, Naboth. Ahimelech of Nob was murdered not by order of an evil Queen, but an evil King—and his orders were carried out by Doeg, Saul's herdsman. Thus, just as fruitless sons murdered a fruitful heir (Naboth), an *evil* shepherd murdered the *holy* shepherd of God's people (Ahimelech).

We should note another significant Hebrew etymology in Naboth's place of origin: the Scripture refers to him as Naboth the Jezreelite (I Kings 21.1). Jezreel (יזרעאל) literally means "God sows." Naboth was slain because he detested that which was evil and sought to do good, desiring to obey the commandments of God. In truth, he became a seed sown for righteousness—for the sake of the inheritance, his vineyard.

We may also consider how, perhaps, Naboth stands as foreshadowing, a type and shadow of the righteous remnant of the last days, who will not abandon their God-given inheritance—the land covenant—and who will be persecuted for this by the spirit of Jezebel (Babylon the Great), the controlling religious spirit who calls for Israel to abandon its inheritance and divide its land. I this the same evil queen who manipulates the kings of the world, the spirit of Ahab within the evil political powers whom she rides? It is also fascinating to note that the final battle of Armageddon, the last battle for inheritance, will also be fought in the valley of Jezreel. Here, God Himself will defend the covenant He has made with His children. (Judges 6:33, Judges 1:27, I Kings 9:15, Revelation 16:14).

Inheritance—God's glory—cannot be sold, divided or traded for peace—and must be guarded with our very lives. The inheritance of Naboth's vineyard, in fact, cost him his life to protect. Covenantal inheritance must be honored at all cost. Scripture reveals that satan comes to "steal, kill and destroy"

(John 10:10) the treasures of the Kingdom which we have legal right to possess. The enemy will attempt to destroy all of our inheritance if we do not actively receive and defend what God longs to release to us.

How do we defend this inheritance? By standing on the promises of God—our testimony—and the Blood of the Lamb.

Our birthright is precious to God because it was purchased by Christ at Calvary. Although it is necessary to battle for our birthright and spiritual inheritance, never question for a moment that Almighty God is deeply concerned about our receiving inheritance and legacy—and keeping it.

Ahab

THE WICKED, CONTROLLED MAN
THE POUTING POTENTATE

That night in East Texas years ago, Dr. Lee offered one of the best descriptions I have ever heard of this wicked man Ahab. He described Ahab as a "vile human toad who squatted upon the throne of his nation—the worst of Israel's kings." Although King Ahab commanded his nation's wealth and army, he lacked all control over his own lusts and appetites. The prophet Isaiah was right to declare that *the bed is too short and the cover too small to conceal our sins* (Isaiah 28:20)—and Ahab certainly could not hide his. His rich robes did little to cover his evil, troubled heart.

When righteousness rules a nation, Scripture reminds us, peace and prosperity reign. When wickedness rules, however, the nation is like a troubled sea, tossed and turning. King Ahab's subjects considered him a mean, selfish despot, the curse of his country. Ahab may have been crowned "king" and given a scepter, but he was controlled by a demonic woman who dominated him for most of his life, reducing him to no more than a puppet. Ahab was just a tool in Jezebel's hands.

In I Kings 21:25-26, Ahab is described as being "stirred" by Jezebel to act "abominably":

> But there was no one like Ahab who sold himself to do wickedness in the sight of the LORD, because Jezebel his wife stirred him up. And he behaved very abominably in following idols, according to all that the Amorites had done, whom the LORD had cast out before the children of Israel.

In I Kings 16:33, we read that Ahab *provoked* the Lord with his actions—more than any king who ruled before him:

> And Ahab made a wooden image. Ahab did more to provoke the LORD God of Israel to anger than all the kings of Israel who were before him.

The Hebrew root translated provoke (נאץ or *na'ats*) is an extremely strong verb. *Na'ats* suggests that Ahab actively *rejected* God—*na'ats* meaning *to despise, to condemn* and *to reject with contempt and derision*. The Lord used this same term *na'ats* when He asked Moses, "How long will this people *provoke* me?" Ahab did not just provoke God's anger: he *despised* God, turning his back on Him with pure contempt. In his contempt for God, Ahab made a "wooden image," a carving of *Asherah*, or a Canaanite goddess—the wife of a war god, symbolized by the bare trunk of a tree. Such was the wickedness of King Ahab, who asked to purchase Naboth's inheritance.

Ahab feasted on the finest food and drank the best wine the world could supply—with a host of servants for every whim—but as he reclined at his banqueting table, he possessed a starved soul. He lived in extravagant palaces, luxurious within and without, yet he tormented himself with his greed and lust for *one small tract of land*, Naboth's vineyard.

Naboth's quick, firm, refusal unsettled Ahab's desires and plans. Disappointed and despondent, the pouting king returned home:

> And Ahab came into his house heavy and displeased because of the word which Naboth the Jezreelite had spoken to him: for he had said, I will not give thee the inheritance of my fathers. And he laid him down upon his bed, and turned away his face, and would eat no bread.
>
> (I Kings 21:4)

What a pouting potentate! What a ridiculous, pathetic scene! A king acting like a spoiled child, unable to function, driven to his bed in a petty rage. Ahab's victories over the Syrians were known in many lands—but now the victor was a slave to himself, whining like a sick hound. Servants brought him meals but he "would eat no bread." His spirit was in bondage, mired in self-pity. Ahab had actually lost nothing: he had land and houses aplenty. No one had injured him. No one had made attempts on his life. Yet this king, with his great army and fat treasury, was acting like a fool—all for a little spot of grass outside his own vast pastures. Here, so clearly illustrated, we see that one of the most deadly demons is *self-centeredness*.

How tragic that we attempt to satisfy the gnawing hungers of our hearts with the temporal trinkets of this life!

How we need to take heed to the warning of our Lord and Savior Christ Jesus, "Beware! Don't be greedy for what you don't have. Real life is not measured by how much we own" (Luke 12:15, NLT).

Christ Jesus reminds us that our success is not in the size of our material assets: "For what is a man profited if he should gain the whole world and lose his own soul?" (Matthew 16:26).

Surely King Ahab had lost his.

Many in our time and culture suffer from a profound lack of true contentment. Godly contentment can only be found through a daily, *living encounter* with Christ Jesus. The most content people on earth are those who know Christ, who are seeking to put Him first in their lives and to devote themselves to serving others. In other words, "Godliness with contentment is great gain" (I Titus 6:6).

The Greek meaning of *contentment*, ατάρκεια or *autarkeia*, describes *a perfect condition of life in which no help is necessary*. The term means *having all that is needed*—more specifically, *a mind contented with its lot*.

This mirrors a definition of *justice*, which, in its Hebrew root, can be described as *rain in just measure, as the ground naturally requires*. When our hearts receive all that they require, in just measure, they rest content. To rise up as a holy priesthood and cry out for the salvation of others is to ask that there be "rain in *just* measure," the rain of His justice for individuals, families and nations—their inheritance.

What is the *opposite* of contentment in our just measure in Christ? Murmuring and complaining in the desert—about how unfair life is. But consider this truth: it is a *sin against* God to murmur and complain, on either a personal or a national level. In the wilderness, the people "murmured" against Moses and they failed to enter the Promised Land of their inheritance. This Hebrew term *murmur* (לון or *luwn*) not only means to *complain* or *grumble* but it also translated as *lodge, remain and abide*. To murmur during our journey—in a spirit of *fear* (as Doeg, who murdered the brother of the King) or *unbelief* (as unfruitful Belial, who murdered the heir of the vineyard)—is *to choose to abide* in the wilderness, to refuse to enter the Promised Land. We must recognize the important difference between murmuring against God in unbelief and crying out for justice in faith, standing on His promises.

Jezebel

THE WICKED, CONTROLLING WOMAN
THE PERSONIFICATION OF PERVERSITY

The Hebrew name *Jezebel* literally means *unchaste* or *Baal is husband to*. The word Baal, in early Hebrew culture, simply meant "Lord," and was formerly used to identify the God of Abraham. By the time of Ahab, however, *Baal* referred exclusively to the Phoenician sun-god, to whom first-born children were sacrificed by fire. Jezebel was a daughter of a king, Ethbaal, King of Tyre (I Kings 16:31), "Ethbaal" literally meaning *living with Baal and enjoying his help*. Jezebel married another king, Ahab, becoming a king's daughter and a king's wife, an idolatrous daughter-wife to an idolatrous king of an idolatrous people. She not only engaged with her maidens in introducing Baal worship into Samaria, but also in worshipping Ashtoreth, the Phoenician goddess of war and fertility, also worshipped by the Philistines. The Lord called these practices "abominations" (II Kings 23:13).

Jezebel was the personification of perversity. She led her people into the worst obscenities, uncleanness, and sensuality. Masterful, determined and ruthless, Jezebel hated anyone who spoke against or refused to worship her pagan gods. Not only was she was a *patroness of idolatry* (I Kings 18:19), but she was *vengeful* (I Kings 19:2), *murderous* (I Kings 21:5–13) and *vain* (I Kings 9:30). Above all, she *incited Ahab* to evil (1Kings 21:25). Jezebel was substantially more daring and reckless in her wickedness than her wicked husband Ahab. Her evil genius was responsible for wreaking havoc and devising death.

In all recorded history and literature, it is difficult to find another woman as evil as Jezebel. She was as brazen in her lewdness as Cleopatra. She possessed the subtle, perverse scheming of Lady Macbeth. Her beauty incited the same adulterous treachery as Potiphar's wife (Gen. 39:7–20). She possessed the whimsical wickedness of Catherine of Russia and the devilish infamy of Madame Pompadour. Yet Jezebel was truly in a league all her own, more wicked than them all. Only the demons of hell can so empower such a person.

When Ahab sulked and would "eat no bread," his servants quickly reported to Jezebel. Provoked by the news that her husband would not eat, that he had gone to bed when it was not bedtime, Jezebel hurried to investigate. She found Ahab pouting, his face to the wall, his eyes red, his heart set in wicked rebellion.

In a voice of "sweet" solicitation, Jezebel sought the reason for her husband's anger: "Why is your spirit so sad, that you eat no bread?" (I Kings 21:5).

The king whined in response, "Because I spoke unto Naboth the Jezreelite, and said unto him, Give me thy vineyard for money; or else, if it please thee, I will give thee another vineyard for it: and he answered, I will not give thee my vineyard" (I Kings 21:6).

Hear Jezebel's derisive, sarcastic laugh as it rings out in the palace: "With her razor sharp tongue, she prods Ahab as an ox driver prods with sharp goad the ox which does not want to press his neck into the yoke, or as one whips with a rawhide a stubborn mule."

She ridicules her king, reminding him that he is nothing more than a cowardly buffoon. Her sarcastic words wound like daggers. What fury in the shrieking of her rebuke! One can only imagine the bitterness in the teasing taunts she hurled at him for his timidity. She stands not as a faithful, comforting wife, but as a woman controlled by demonic forces. Hear her hiss out her mocking words: "Are you not the king of this country?" she chides. "Can you not command and have it done? You are crying like a baby and will not eat anything because you do not have courage to take a bit of land."

She taunts, jeering the king of Israel:

> And Jezebel his wife said unto him, Do you now govern the kingdom of Israel? arise, and eat bread, and let your heart be merry: I will give you the vineyard of Naboth the Jezreelite.
>
> —I Kings 21:7

Ahab knew Jezebel well enough to know that she would do her best—or her worst—to keep her wicked promise. Indeed, when true authority is missing, Jezebel rules: there can be no controlling Jezebel spirit without a cowardly spirit of Ahab. The cry of our heart must be: *Lord, let the men of God arise!*

Who can so inspire a man to noble purposes as a noble woman? Who can so thoroughly degrade a man as an evil wife? Consider two Scriptures: "And Ahab the son of Omri did evil in the sight of the Lord above all that were before him" (I Kings 16:30) and (Elijah speaking), "You have sold yourself to work evil in the sight of the

Lord" (I Kings 21:20). Behind both statements is another: "Whom Jezebel his wife stirred up." Jezebel was the devil's grindstone which sharpened Ahab's wicked weapons.

Search the pages of the Scripture and study history: the truth that the spiritual life of a nation, city, town, school, church or home *never rises higher than the spiritual life of women.* When women fall morally and spiritually, men fail morally and spiritually. A woman without a firm spiritual foundation in her heart is like a rainbow without color. What a terrible tragedy when any woman thinks more of pearls than principles of righteous adornment. When women take the downward road, men travel with them—yet a godly woman secures a healthy, spiritual home (Proverbs 31).

What is the relationship between *purity* and *God's justice*?

In Lamentations 4:7, we read how the "Nazarites were purer than snow"—bright, clean, shining and washed—consecrated unto God by the good works they performed. Christ fulfills this cleansing and separation once and for all, purifying us by baptism and imputing righteousness or justice—through His Cross. We are carriers of His justice, having been born again. Our inheritance is His justice, and this justice cannot be taken from us, no matter the circumstance.

Truly, purity is a vehicle for the glory of God to be inherited and secured. And here we turn to the voice of righteousness, the voice of Elijah and the Body of Christ.

Elijah
THE HOLY, HUMBLE PROPHET
THE VOICE OF RIGHTEOUSNESS

*E*ven when wickedness seems to run unchecked, God always has a people with clean hands and pure hearts, a remnant called to confront a contaminated culture. Elijah the Tishbite was such a man, chosen to live and prophesy during the reign of this most wicked Jezebel and her puppet King Ahab.

Elijah's name, or *'el-yaah'*, literally means *my God is Jehovah or Yah(u) is God*. Knowing his God and the glorious past of God's people, this holy prophet of Jehovah must have been filled with horror when he learned of the rank heathenism, fierce cruelties and reeking licentiousness of Ahab's idolatrous capital. Elijah lived at a time when tens of thousands of God's people had forsaken His covenants, thrown down God's altars and slain His prophets (I Kings 19:10). Holy anger burned within Elijah like unquenchable fire, fanned by the holy jealousy of God for His beloved Bride.

Unlike the wicked king Ahab, this humble prophet ate the most meager fare and wore the roughest clothes. Underneath his ragged garments, however, a righteous and courageous heart throbbed for the glory of God to return to the nation. Elijah did not eat his food from fine tableware as Ahab did; he ate bird's food and widow's portions—but he was a spiritual champion, a strong oak of righteousness. He wrestled with the pagan giants of his day without bending or breaking, speaking against the rising apostasy of his day. Rest assured that God is again calling forth His dread champions that will stand tall calling the nations back to purity and purpose.

Despite his public calling, Elijah loved solitude, spending much time alone, often attended by the invisible hosts of God. He lamented only when God's cause seemed to falter. He passed from earth without dying, into celestial glory (2 Kings 2)—and with Elijah's passing, Elisha received the "double portion." This "portion" in Hebrew, פה or *peh*, literally means *mouth* and suggests *authority* or *commandment*. The word "portion" derives from the root word פאה or *pa'ah*, an extremely strong verb meaning *to cleave or break in pieces, to shatter, to scatter into corners*. The "portion" that the spirit of Elijah released with his passing is the *unstoppable mouth* which scatters evil—the same spirit that John the Baptist carried as he preached, that also provoked the spirit of Jezebel and led to his beheading. This "portion" of the spirit of Elijah is the prophetic mouth of authority that speaks God's Word and shatters injustice.

Note also that this same word *peh* is used for *the edge of the sword*: "And Nob, the city of the priests, smote them with *the edge of the sword*" (I Sam. 22:19).

Everywhere courage is admired, manhood honored and service appreciated, Elijah is honored as one of our greatest heroes and one of heaven's greatest saints. He was a seer who saw clearly. He was a great heart who felt deeply. He was a hero who dared valiantly, a prophet of God who stood strong against all odds.

Our times call for bold, brave Christians like Elijah who will confront the carnality of our culture, "coming out from among them" and shining as beacons of hope and love in an ever-darkening world. May God release men and women today with this same unquenchable zeal for justice!

PART TWO
The Rights to Naboth's Vineyard
THE BATTLE FOR GOD'S JUSTICE

> And it came to pass after these things that Naboth the Jezreelite had a vineyard which was in Jezreel, next to the palace of Ahab king of Samaria. So Ahab spoke to Naboth, saying, "Give me your vineyard, that I may have it for a vegetable garden, because it is near, next to my house; and for it I will give you a vineyard better than it. Or, if it seems good to you, I will give you its worth in money.
>
> —I Kings 21:1–2

King Ahab was actually within his rights in offering to buy Naboth's vineyard. He seemingly had no intention of cheating Naboth out of his vineyard or of murdering him to get it. Ahab offered Naboth "the worth of it in money," a fair price for the vineyard—or, if Naboth preferred, *a better vineyard*: "I will give thee for it a better vineyard than it." It was a fair-and-square deal. Under ordinary circumstances, we would have expected Naboth to disregard his sentimental attachment to his inheritance in order to please his king—especially when the king had no desire to swindle him.

Ahab, however, had not expected Naboth's reluctance to sell. We will do well to study the motivations of Naboth's heart: why did he love his vineyard? What made it *abhorrent* for him to sell it for gain? Naboth knew that the Lord of Heaven had given him this right to possess his vineyard.

He knew the land was his true inheritance, his glory, and that it must be protected at all costs.

Every Israelite believed that in *every* land-holding transaction there was another, more authoritative party, God Himself, "who made the heavens and the earth." Throughout Judah and Israel, Jehovah was the true Owner of the soil. Every tribe received its territory and every family its inheritance by lot from Him—with the added condition that the land should never, *under any circumstances*, be sold, traded or divided.

In our time of political pressures and boundary disputes, we must remember that God has promised—by Holy Covenant—to give the land of Israel to the Jewish nation *forever*.

Israel *must not trade* its land for peace, *negotiate* its worth for political purposes or *divide* this holy inheritance in response to pressures from enemies.

The land was given to the Jews forever, an inheritance sealed by God's covenant to Abram, renamed Abraham.

The first time God promises the land to Abram and his descendents was in Genesis 12:7:

> Then the LORD appeared to Abram and said, "To your

descendants I will give this land." And there he built an altar to the LORD, who had appeared to him.

In the next chapter, God *shows* Abram his inheritance and tells him to walk through the land to claim it (Gen. 13:15–17):

> And the LORD said to Abram, after Lot had separated from him: "Lift your eyes now and look from the place where you are—northward, southward, eastward, and westward; for all the land which you see I give to you and your descendants forever. And I will make your descendants as the dust of the earth; so that if a man could number the dust of the earth, then your descendants also could be numbered. Arise, walk in the land through its length and its width, for I give it to you."

The Lord then formalized Abram's inheritance by cutting a covenant with him, promising that the land would be his inheritance *forever* (Gen. 15:17–18):

> And it came to pass, when the sun went down and it was dark, that behold, there appeared a smoking oven and a burning torch that passed between those pieces. On the same day the LORD made a covenant with Abram, saying: "To your descendants I have given this land, from the river of Egypt to the great river, the River Euphrates…"

The Abrahamic covenant was an everlasting *land covenant* between God and Abraham. God was asking Abraham not to give away the land of his inheritance. Abraham was to seal this covenant with circumcision as the visible sign of his abiding by this promise (Genesis 17):

> And I will establish My covenant between Me and you and your descendants after you in their generations, for an everlasting covenant, to be God to you and your descendants after you. Also I give to you and your descendants after you the land in which you are a stranger, all the land of Canaan, as an everlasting possession; and I will be their God."
>
> And God said to Abraham: "As for you, you shall keep My covenant, you and your descendants after you throughout their generations. This is My covenant which you shall keep, between Me and you and your descendants after you: Every male child among you shall be circumcised…"

In Lev. 25:23 and Numbers 36:7–9, we discover divine truth and extremely important revelation concerning our rightful inheritance. The land shall not be sold *forever*:

> For the land is mine; for you are strangers and sojourners with Me…So shall not the inheritance of the children of Israel remove from tribe to tribe: for every one of the children of Israel shall keep himself to the inheritance of the tribe of his fathers…but every one of the tribes of the children of Israel shall keep himself to his own inheritance.

In these passages we learn that the permanent sale of the paternal inheritance was *forbidden by law*. Ahab forgot—if he had ever really known—that, for Naboth, to sell or to swap his vineyard would be a denial of his allegiance to the true religion. Although Naboth was Ahab's nearest neighbor and the subject of the king, he stood firmly on his religious rights, informed by his honoring of *Torah*, or Jewish law. What outstanding courage it took to refuse the king's request and stand for righteousness—Naboth's inheritance and his legacy to his children's children.

Because his vineyard was close to the king's palace, Naboth must have been an eye-witness to what took place within its borders—debase idolatry. Perhaps he feared that his little plot of ground, so rich in prayer and fellowship, sanctified with sweet and holy memories, would be contaminated and cursed if it came into the hands of Jezebel. With "the courage of a lioness that protects it cub," he took his stand against the king's proposal.

Today many suffer because of lost legacy and stolen inheritances. We, too, must be of good courage and battle for what God has given to us—as we are encouraged to do in the book of Joshua. We are to *go in* and possess our inheritance, dispossessing it of everything previously owned by the enemy.

> Now therefore, arise, go over this Jordan, you and all this people, to the land which I am giving to them—the children of Israel. Every place that the sole of your foot will tread upon I have given you, as I said to Moses. From the wilderness and this Lebanon as far as the great river, the River Euphrates, all the land of the Hittites, and to the Great Sea toward the going down of the sun, shall be your territory…Be strong and of good courage, for to this people you shall divide as an inheritance the land which I swore to their fathers to give them.
>
> —Joshua 1:2–6

Naboth, with much fear of God and little fear of man, squared his shoulders and declared: "The Lord forbid it me, that I should give the inheritance of my fathers unto you" (I Kings 21:3). True to the teachings of his father, and out of a profound loyalty to the covenant God of Israel, Naboth believed that he held the land because *it was promised to him by God*. Naboth's father, grandfather and grandfather's father had possessed the land before him. His refusal to negotiate with Ahab was quick, firm and final.

The spirit of Ahab and the spirit of Jezebel have always come against the spirit of the prophet—Naboth, John the Baptist—and his inheritance, the land of Israel and its King. *It is the spirit of antichrist that wants to sell and divide the covenant land*. In 2 Thessalonians 2:8, we read that it is the "lawless one," or the Torah-less one, the antichrist, the one who *breaks the covenants* of Moses and Abraham. In Daniel 11:28, this antichrist is described as one "against the holy covenant." This is the same spirit in Daniel 11:39, who will *divide the land for gain*. In the book of Joel we read that God will *judge* the nations who "divided up My land":

> I will also gather all nations, and bring them down to
> the Valley of Jehoshaphat; and I will enter into judgment
> with them there on account of My people, My heritage
> Israel, whom they have scattered among the nations;
> they have also divided up My land.
> —Joel 3:2

Isaiah the prophet used the term *vineyard* to represent the people of Israel. To refuse to abandon his vineyard (the Hebrew term כרם or *kerem* also referring to an *olive yard*), Naboth is refusing to abandon the nation of Israel and, perhaps, on a deeper reading, the prophetic grove of Gethsemane, where the battle for our eternal inheritance was fought—and won.

The Lying Letters
JUSTICE PERVERTED, RIGHTEOUSNESS MOCKED

Jezebel wrote letters to the elders of Jezreel in which she made a subtle yet definite declaration that a terrible sin had been committed in their city. She wrote in Ahab's name and secured the letters with Ahab's seal, working behind the scenes. She then dispatched the forged, sealed documents to the elders and nobles in the city:

> Proclaim a fast, and set Naboth on high among the people: and set two men, sons of Belial, before him, to bear witness against him, saying, "You did blaspheme God and the king." And then carry him out, and stone him, that he may die.
>
> —I Kings 21:8–10

These letters were a hideous mockery of true religion: if Jezebel could have Naboth convicted of blasphemy by divine law, then, by law, the property of the blasphemer went to the crown. Not only would the letters secure the land, but the letters were a literal death warrant for innocent Naboth, sealed with Ahab's ring (I Kings 21:8).

Fasting had always been a sign of humiliation before God, of humbling oneself in the dust before the "high and lofty One that inhabits eternity." Calling a fast, according to tradition, signified that the community was under the anger of God because of a grave crime committed by one of its members—a crime to be exposed and punished. The fast also called for work to cease so that the citizens would have time to attend public gatherings.

When Jezebel orders the elders to "*set Naboth on high*," she refers to the "height" of the bar of justice, not the seat of honor. "On high" described the seat of the accused: Naboth was put where every eye could watch him closely and keenly observe his bearing under the accusation. "And set two men, base fellows, before him." Jezebel was in fact breaking the law in bringing about Naboth's death in a legal way! The law required two witnesses in all cases where the punishment was death. "At the mouth of two witnesses, or three witnesses, shall he…be put to death" (Deut. 17:6). The witnesses required by Jezebel were men of no character, men who would take bribes and swear to any lie for gain.

The Scriptures read: "And let them bear witness against him." In other words, the two men of Belial were to put Naboth "out of the way" by judicial murder, not by private assassination. "And then carry him *out*, and stone him, that he may die." A criminal was not to be executed within a city, as that would defile it. (Thus Christ was crucified outside the walls of Jerusalem). Obviously, Jezebel took it for granted that Naboth would be condemned.

While Naboth worked in his vineyard, the letters arrived at Jezreel. One evening, while Naboth talked at the cottage door with his sons or neighbors, the message was delivered to the elders of the city. A fast had been proclaimed, he heard—proclaimed because God had been offended by some crime and that His wrath must be appeased—and he himself, ignorant of any offense toward God or the king, was to be set in the place of the accused, a criminal, "on high among the people."

Here we have a model for what is transpiring in our current world scene—a false religious system, *a spirit of religion*, controlling a corrupt political system, employing its name and authority to rob God's people of their covenant land, usurp their civil freedoms and set the innocent in the seat of the accused.

May the priests and prophets of the Body of Christ rise up to defend our inheritance, the covenant land, and cry out for justice for the oppressed!

The Death of Naboth
THE WHEELS OF JUSTICE BEGIN TO TURN

The household of Naboth must have been extremely concerned when the family realized that Naboth was to be "set on high," even in the "seat of the accused" before the bar of "justice"—because of a vicious message *calling religion to attest to a lie*. And what excitement there must have been in the city when the elders and nobles "fastened the minds" of the people upon the fast, as if some great calamity were overhanging the city. Curious throngs hurried to the fast to see the accused, the man who brought forth the wrath of God.

The rulers of Jezreel—in dread of offending one whose revenge they knew was terrible, or eager to do a service—carried out Jezebel's instructions to the letter. No doubt she had tested their character as her "butcher boys" in the slaughter of the prophets of the Lord.

And they obeyed! "And there came in two men, children of Belial, and sat down before him" (I Kings 21:13). The devil's hawks—perjurers—were ready to bring death to God's harmless dove. "And the men of Belial witnessed against him, even against Naboth, in the presence of the people, saying, 'Naboth did blaspheme God and the king'" (I Kings 21:13).

The name *Belial*, speaks of worthlessness and wickedness, a person or people with no true uprightness of character or fruitfulness. How easy for the wicked to cast stones at the upright.

Suddenly, wicked hands seized Naboth, dragging him from his home, through the throngs of onlookers, to a place outside the city walls, beating his body with stones—his innocent blood splattering the witnesses. The devout Naboth's arms are broken, his ribs crushed. His mauled body becomes, at last, perfectly still.

Perhaps we can hear the angels of God crying out, "Let justice roll down like a river and justice like a mighty stream" (Amos 5:24)!

We learn from II Kings 9:26 that, by the law of those days, his innocent sons were also accused; to prevent them from claiming the inheritance of the field, they, too, were slain.

The covenant land, left without its rightful heirs, reverted to corrupt political and religious powers.

Consequently, Naboth fell—not by the king's hand, or so it seemed, but by the condemnation of his fellow citizens. No doubt Naboth's righteous lifestyle made him unpopular in "progressive" Jezreel. Jezebel carried out her purpose in a perfectly legal and orderly way—in a "democratic" manner—a fine picture of *dictatorship by democracy*. When the "patriotic citizens" of Jezreel had left the bodies of Naboth and his sons to be devoured by the wild dogs, "Then they sent to Jezebel, saying, Naboth is stoned, and is dead" (I Kings 21:14).

Given Jezebel's nature, she probably received the tragic news of Naboth's death with devilish delight. What did it matter to her that outside the city walls the dogs licked the blood of this godly man?

Did she care that Jehovah God had been defied, His commandments broken, His altars splattered with pagan mud, His holy Name profaned?

What did she care if justice had been outraged? She had gained the little plot of land close to the palace! Her test in getting the vineyard was a decided triumph.

In her words and manner there was satanic elation. When Jezebel heard that Naboth had been stoned to death, she told the king to "Arise, take possession of the vineyard of Naboth the Jezreelite, which be refused to give thee for money: for Naboth is not alive, but dead" (I Kings 21:15)!

Where is God's justice at this moment of Naboth's death? Did satan have the upper hand?

Hear a lesson of immense value: Naboth's love for the land was intimately connected to his love for his inheritance. This love for his inheritance was noble and true, to be sure; however, there exists a love of even greater—priceless—worth. He loved the *Torah*, the Word of God, and committed himself to abide by the covenant... willing to give his life for the land.

Hear this profound truth: Love was fulfilled and made complete in Naboth. How is this possible? Naboth stepped into the *original intent* of the Word of God for his life. Naboth's destiny was to become a type and shadow of the righteous remnant of the last days who abides by the land covenant. Naboth is also a type and shadow of Christ Himself. Notice the similarities: the mock judicial trial, evil religious men plotting against him, being dragged outside the city to die an innocent man. The Messiah, Christ Jesus, gave His life for us, His inheritance.

Naboth was made complete in love because he fulfilled the word of the God, which required that Naboth, prophet and priest, offer his life to protect the Inheritance as a type of Christ. Just as Christ triumphed in life through His death, so Naboth.

It is the plan and purpose of God that we are *always the victors, and never—never—the victim*. We would do well to remember the meaning of the word *martyr—a witness*, one who avers what he himself has seen or heard. Naboth served as a witness to God's unchanging covenant, his God-given inheritance which could not be sold, traded or divided, and was martyred for his faith.

The Loss of the Vineyard
JUSTICE PROMISED, HOPE ASSURED

How Jezebel must have paraded with pride before Ahab, announcing that the vineyard was now his…for nothing!

Imagine her rueful sarcasm when she made it known that she had succeeded where Ahab had failed. Enduring her taunts, Ahab "rose up to go down," from Samaria to Jezreel. "And it came to pass, when Ahab heard that Naboth was dead, that Ahab rose up to go down to the vineyard of Naboth the Jezreelite, to take possession of it" (I Kings 21:16). Ahab gave orders to his royal wardrobe keeper to get out his king's clothes, because he had a little "business" trip to make, to survey property that had come to him by his wife's shrewdness!

Naboth, the good man who "feared the lord," was dead—and this king expresses no condemnation of the awful conspiracy and tragic murder. By the evil genius of his queen, he could "receive the benefit of [Naboth's] dying."

The Justice of God

Notice at this point that *not one noble or elder* had divulged the terrible secret which had given the semblance of legality to the atrocious wrongdoing. When good men do not cry out against evil, wickedness surely increases. Indeed, prophetic voices *must not be silent* as darkness grows darker. God warns the prophet Ezekiel of the consequences of this disobedience:

> When I say to the wicked, 'O wicked man, you shall
> surely die!' and you do not speak to warn the wicked
> from his way, that wicked man shall die in his iniquity;
> but his blood I will require at your hand.
> —Ezekiel 33:8

Ahab, rejoicing in getting what he wanted, gave orders to the livery stables to ready his royal chariot for an unexpected trip. Jehu and Bidkar, the royal charioteers, prepared the great horses such as kings had in those days. Jehu, the speed-breaking driver of his day, rode a gilded chariot, his outriders dressed in gorgeous garments. In an interesting parallel, we see this same decadence today, with corrupt leaders of nations, gangs and corporations driving about in extremely expensive cars, flying in personal jets for mere pleasure—yet none of this glamour can cover the darkness of a sinful heart. Just as in the day of wicked king Ahab!

At this same time, the prophet of God is sent on his divine mission with God's warning: "You shall speak to him, saying…"

> Then the word of the Lord came to Elijah the Tishbite,
> saying, "Arise, go down to meet Ahab king of Israel,
> who lives in Samaria. There he is, in the vineyard of
> Naboth, where he has gone down to take possession of
> it. You shall speak to him, saying, 'Thus says the Lord:
> Have you murdered and also taken possession?' And

you shall speak to him, saying, 'Thus says the Lord: In the place where dogs licked the blood of Naboth, dogs shall lick your blood, even yours.'" And of Jezebel also spake the Lord, saying, "The dogs shall eat Jezebel by the wall of Jezreel"

—I Kings 21:17–19

En route to Jezreel to take Naboth's land, perhaps the charioteers' cracking whips attract attention. Does anyone along the dusty roads cry out for justice?

Imagine the dust clouds rising from the racing wheels. Can we see anyone raising a hand to stop the charging horses?

Soon everyone in Jezreel knows the king is arriving to possess Naboth's vineyard—and most who stand along the road wrongly believe it was possessed with fairness and justice. Indeed, the gilded chariot reflects the sun brightly—all seems right and just—but few know that the souls of those riding are stained with the blood of a martyr. Jezebel and Ahab paid for the land with the blood of its rightful owner.

Will they learn that sin buys pleasure at the high price of peace?

Once the Lord spoke to me saying "Bobby, these sounds are sometimes very faint—almost muted on earth—yet they are heard extremely clear in heaven."

I asked Him, "What sounds, Lord?"

He replied, "The sound of the breaking of a heart and the shattering of dreams."

These sounds may be coming from your own broken heart and shattered dreams. Right now, you may feel that no one understands the profound hurts and devastating losses and disappointments you are facing.

You may have been robbed of your inheritance—your family, your joy, your peace, your land.

You may feel as though the enemy has taken complete possession of your life, stealing what is rightfully yours, the provisions and promises of God. I assure you: *God truly knows your pain*. He is constant on His watch for you, acting on your behalf. He *will* vindicate you and redeem your life—and will not delay.

The Alarming Appearance
THE WORD OF JUSTICE ARRIVES

The furious 20-mile journey from Samaria to Jezreel is completed. Jehu the charioteer pulls up to the gate of the vineyard and secures the horses. The harnesses are heavy with sweat, the horses' breathing like massive bellows—brute beasts unaware of the evil they're aiding. Bidkar opens the chariot door.

Ahab steps onto Naboth's inheritance.

The enemy has seemed to take possession of God's covenant land, the land that should have been secured *forever*.

No doubt Ahab sees Naboth's footprints in the soft soil; close by, perhaps he sees the smaller footprints of Naboth's wife and children.

Naboth's pruning hook is still leaning against the vines.

The coveted vineyard is now Ahab's, thanks to the wicked scheming of his queen.

For the righteous, all hope seems to be lost.

THE JUSTICE OF GOD

The wicked king struts along the borders of his conquered land, perhaps planning how his royal gardeners will pull up the vines, carve up the territory, caring nothing for the lifelong labors of the previous owner—disregarding the invasion of covenant land.

While Ahab surveys his new possession, what might grip his heart with sudden fear?

A shadow falls across his path—and suddenly, like an apparition from the other world, Elijah stands before Ahab!

Elijah, prophet of the living God, holds a staff and wears sheepskin, a leather girdle about his loins. His cheeks are tanned and weather beaten, but his eyes are fiery coals burning with righteous indignation.

Ahab had not seen Elijah for five years—and no doubt assumed the prophet had been silenced by Jezebel. Now the prophet *boldly confronts* the wicked king with a death warrant from the Lord God Almighty. Suddenly Ahab's face goes white. His lips quiver. He had journeyed to take possession of his coveted garden, but there he is—face-to-face with *righteousness* and *justice*.

The vineyard had become a courtroom. The God of righteousness and justice was about to pass sentence upon Ahab.

The heart of the wicked trembles in horror as prophet and king stand eye-to-eye. Showing no honor to the prophet of God, "Ahab said to Elijah, Hast thou found me, O mine enemy?" (I Kings 21:20).

Elijah answers, the prophet's eyes burning Ahab's guilty soul: "I have found you: because you have sold yourself to work evil in the sight of the Lord."

Every word a thunderbolt, Elijah continues:

> Hast thou killed and also taken possession? Thus says the Lord, "In the place where dogs licked the blood of Naboth shall dogs lick thy blood, even thine…Behold,

I will bring evil upon thee, and will take away thy posterity…and will make thine house like the house of Jeroboam the son of Nebat, and like the house of Baasha the son of Ahijah, for the provocation wherewith thou hast provoked me to anger, and made Israel to sin!"
—I Kings 21:19, 21, 22

Like a terrible scourge, Elijah presses on:

"And of Jezebel also spake the Lord, saying, 'The dogs shall eat Jezebel by the wall of Jezreel. Him that dies of Ahab in the city the dogs shall eat: and him that dies in the field shall the fowls of the air eat'"
—I Kings 21:23, 24

Appearing and disappearing quickly, as was his custom, Elijah went his way, leaving Ahab to cower in his wake.

Ahab had sold himself for nothing, as Achan did—for a burial robe and a useless bar of gold—and as Judas did—for thirty pieces of silver that so burned his soul that he found relief only in the noose.

God had spoken to Ahab: would it come to pass? As the king returned to Jezebel, the horses' hooves pounded the prophet's words into Ahab's guilty soul: "Someday, the dogs will lick thy blood! Someday, the dogs will eat Jezebel by the ramparts of Jezreel."

Never forget: the words that depart from God's mouth will not return to Him empty, but will bring to pass *what He has planned*.

Never forget: God is not mocked.

PART THREE
Redeeming Naboth's Vineyard
THE COMING JUDGEMENT DAY

To be sure, Divine Justice is written in the constitution of God's universe: the retributive providence of God is as real and certain as the law of gravity. A.W. Tozer made this strong statement:

> In human affairs, many an innocent man has been hanged. Many a life-termer has died in gray pallor behind prison walls, while the rascal who actually committed the crime died in his own bed, surrounded by his friends. But thanks be to God that Jesus is not only our faithful Savior, but our righteous Judge. The eternal truth should either set us at ease or send us to our knees!

The knowledge of the coming Judgment Day is the trust that produces serious, godly believers. Those who put this Day out of mind are usually cold, careless, and indulgent. The fact remains, however, that sometime very soon—sooner than we believe—every person who has ever lived will be gathered to the place of judgment, to be judged by Jesus Christ:

> For we must all appear before the judgment seat of Christ.
> —2 Cor. 5:10

> So then each of us shall give account of himself to God.
> —Romans 14:12

Falling into the Hands of The Living God

PAYDAY WILL COME!

For Ahab and Jezebel, "payday" came as certainly as night follows day, because sin *carries in itself* the seed of its own fatal penalty. God declares the wages of sin is death. The soul that sins *shall* die.

God's justice is meted out for generations. As Scripture explains, "they sow the wind, and reap the whirlwind" (Hosea 8:7)—not only for those who sow, but to their descendents, the curses carried on within the family line. Even though king Ahab repented for his sin against Naboth, the Lord still punished the king's descendents:

> See how Ahab has humbled himself before Me? Because he has humbled himself before Me, I will not bring the calamity in his days. In the days of his son I will bring the calamity on his house.
>
> —I Kings: 21:29

One generation scatters tares and the next generation reaps tares and retribution immeasurable.

To the individual who does not follow God's direction, a terrible "payday" is inevitable; to the nation that does not honor God, payday *will come*. When nations trample on the principles of the Almighty, the result is that the world is beaten with many stripes. We have seen nations slide into Gehenna—and the smoke of their torment has gone up before our eyes day and night.

Indeed, "Ichabod" will be written on the church that soft-pedals unpleasant truths or that does not unwaveringly stand for faith—or for the covenant land given to Israel. The Lord promises in Zechariah 12:9: "And it shall come to pass in that day, that I will seek to destroy all the nations that come against Jerusalem." According to William Koenig in *Eye to Eye: Facing the Consequences of Dividing Israel*:

What do these major-record setting events have in common?

Nine of the ten costliest insurance events in U.S. history
Six of the seven costliest hurricanes in U.S. history
Three of the four largest tornado outbreaks in U.S. history
Nine of the top ten natural disasters in U.S. history
    ranked by FEMA relief costs
The two largest terrorism events in U.S. history

All of these major catastrophes transpired on the very same day or within 24-hours of U.S. presidents Bush, Clinton and Bush applying pressure on Israel to trade her land for promises of "peace and security," sponsoring major "land for peace" meetings, making major public statements pertaining to Israel's covenant land and /or calling for a Palestinian state.

FALLING INTO THE HANDS OF THE LIVING GOD

As never before, we must be bold to stand strong and contend for the covenants and the faith which have been delivered unto us (Jude 3). Knowing God is a God of tender mercy, we also know that it is "a fearful thing to fall into the hands of the living God" (Heb. 10:31).

It is a mistake to think that we can live anyway we choose and expect the grace and mercy of God to continue to cover our failures. We *must* take responsibility and choose to live in such a manner that we are pleasing to the Lord (Col. 1:9-10).

Our constant prayer should be, "Oh, Lord, let my life be pleasing in your sight!" And we must be vigilant to *pray for the peace of Jerusalem*: "Pray for the peace of Jerusalem: they shall prosper that love thee" (Ps. 122:6).

God's Word promises that each of us will give an account for the manner of life we have lived. Yes, we all must face the judgment of God to give an account of the deeds done in our life, whether good or evil (Rom. 2:6). We would be without hope had it not been for the *unfailing love and mercy* of God! He so loved us that He permitted His only Son to take our punishment, thus dying in our place upon the cross. Scripture states that "Greater love has no man than this, that a man lay down his life for his friends" (John 15:13). Saint or sinner we must c*ome boldly to the throne of God's grace and mercy* to find true cleansing for our sin and help in time of need (Heb. 4:16).

We can prostitute God's holy Name if we will—but we are warned that *payday will come*: "The Lord will not hold him guiltless that takes His Name in vain" (Ex. 20:7). We can follow the way of the wicked, but God does not leave us without *warning*:

> He may go after her straightway, as an ox goes to the
> slaughter, or as a fool to the correction of the stocks;
> Till a dart strike through his liver; as a bird haste to the

snare, and knows not that it is for his life…For she has cast down many wounded: yea, many strong men have been slain by her. Her house is the way to hell, going down to the chambers of death.

—Proverbs 7:22, 23, 26, 27

In our day, it seems acceptable to live loose, yet God is calling His people to *holy uprightness of heart and actions*: only in this way can we truly be pleasing in His sight. Many people feel it is right to drink alcohol and even offer the bottle to others, but the certainty of God's warnings is clear: no drunkard "shall inherit the kingdom of God" (I Cor. 6:10).

Indeed, regarding sin, "At the last it bites like a serpent, and stings like an adder." (Proverbs 23:32).

An unknown poet warns those who do not honor God:

You'll pay.
The knowledge of your acts will weigh
Heavier on your mind each day.
The more you climb, the more you gain,
The more you'll feel the nagging strain.

Many find out too late that the pleasures of sin are but for a moment. It is *only* in Christ that true contentment is found. He alone is the Prince of Peace.

Poet Paul Lawrence Dunbar offers these potent words:

This is the price I pay—
Just for one riotous day—
Years of regret and of grief,
And sorrow without relief.
Suffer it I will, my friend,

Suffer it until the end,
Until the grave shall give relief.
Small was the thing I bought,
Small was the thing at best,
Small was the debt, I thought,
But, O God!—the interest.

Hear this bold statement in Job 4:8: "they that plow iniquity, and sow wickedness, reap the same." As a person continues to follow the broad way of sin, refusing to repent and come to Christ, the results will be a price *much higher than anyone could think*— eternal separation from God in hell. None need to reap this harvest! Christ is willing and ready to save any and all who turn by faith to Him (Romans 10:9-13). The way of the transgressor is a very hard way; however, if we turn in faith to Christ, receiving Him as Savior and Lord, we discover that His grace is sufficient for any and all circumstances we encounter.

God calls each of us to repent to turn from our life of sins and shame.

Hear the plea of God's heart in Isaiah 1:18:

Come now, and let us reason together, says the Lord.
Though your sins are like scarlet, they shall be as white
as snow, though they are red like crimson, they shall be
like wool.

When I was pastor of the First Baptist Church in Texas, much of what I preached and taught was broadcast over the radio and television. Most of the responses I received by letter and phone were encouraging—but some were not.

After airing one message about the reality of heaven and God's redemptive mercy, a listener called in. He was in a rage. My first impulse was to retaliate—but the Spirit of God prompted me to just listen to the man. This was not what I wanted to do, but obedience is always the blessed route. I wanted to hang up, but suddenly the man grew silent. The tone of his voice changed and I listened as he choked back tears.

He began to confess the wounds of an unfaithful wife and broken marriage.

In the most humble tone, he finally asked, "Do you think you can help me?" I eagerly scheduled to meet with him.

God, by His great mercy, released healing for this man's heart.

On another occasion, I was about to leave a burn ward during a visit to a large Dallas hospital when I heard someone calling, "Preacher!" I noticed the voice was coming from behind a bed curtain. Opening the curtain, I found a man wrapped head-to-toe in bandages, with just a small opening for his mouth. Even his eyes were wrapped. I could hardly stand the smell of burnt flesh.

In a sad, bitter voice, the man asked, "Why are you here?"

My heart broke for him. "To tell folks that God loves them and has a plan for their lives," I answered.

This suffering man spoke again, his voice having lost some of its edge. "I called for you, sir, because I want you to tell everyone something for me. I want you to tell them—tell them every chance you get—that the devil only pays in counterfeit money."

He told me his story. Addicted to drugs, this desperate sinner was caught in a drug lab that blew up. Most of the flesh on his body was scorched. His eyes had cooked in their sockets.

Scarred and blinded for life, he wanted to warn others of *the evil payback of sin*.

My heart's deepest desire is to persuade every man, woman, boy and girl to believe the truth that satan *always* pays in counterfeit money.

There is truly a *terribly high* price for low living—higher than any of us can imagine.

Sometimes God's judgments are swift and sometimes there seems to be a delay, but never forget that, if the laws of God are broken, there are *always consequences.*

When we next meet King Ahab in Scripture, three years have passed and he is still king. Perhaps Jezebel has been mocking God's prophet Elijah since his appearance in the vineyard. For three years, Jezebel has been taunting her puny puppet king, saying, "I thought Elijah said the dogs were going to lick your blood!" Ahab probably never heard a dog bark during those years that he did not jump in fright. Perhaps he often woke up in a cold sweat after dreaming of his prophesied doom.

The next passage reminds us that no matter how long God is still at work carrying out His plans. One day, Jehoshaphat, king of Judah, visited Ahab:

> And the king of Israel said unto his servants, "Know you that Ramoth in Gilead is ours, and we be still, and take it not out of the hand of the king of Syria?" And he said unto Jehoshaphat, "Will you go with me to battle to Ramoth-gilead?" And Jehoshaphat said to the king of Israel, "I am as you are, my people as your people, my horses as thy horses."
> —I Kings 22:3, 4

> So the king of Israel and Jehoshaphat the king of Judah went up to Ramoth-gilead.
> —I Kings 22:29

After Jehoshaphat had promised to go with him, Ahab had dreadful frightful premonitions. Remember the warning:

> Whoso digs a pit shall fall therein: and he that rolls a stone, it will return upon him.
> —Proverbs 26:27

As he was approaching the scene of action, Ahab's cowardice exerts itself. Hoping to evade the fate predicted for him—remembering Elijah's withering words—Ahab removed his regalia and royal insignia, disguising himself as a common soldier:

> And the king of Israel said unto Jehoshaphat, "I will disguise myself, and enter into the battle; but you put on your robes." And the king of Israel disguised himself, and went into the battle. Now the king of Syria had commanded the thirty-two captains of his chariots, saying, "Fight with no one small or great, but only with the king of Israel."
> —I Kings 22:30–31

King Jehoshaphat was not injured, although he wore his royal clothes:

> And it came to pass, when the captains of the chariots saw Jehoshaphat, that they said, Surely it is the king of Israel. And they turned aside to fight against him: and Jehoshaphat cried out. And it came to pass, when the captains of the chariots perceived that it was not the king of Israel, that they turned back from pursuing him.
> —I Kings 22:32, 33

In ancient warfare, to capture or kill the opposition's king, commander-in-chief or "champion" (e.g., Goliath) often ended the battle then and there. The death of the leader always took the heart out of the common soldier. The Syrian king's command was thus a strategy for winning a quick, decisive victory. The chariot officers at first pursued Jehoshaphat, who would also be in a chariot, with a driver and probably a bowman. Jehoshaphat cried out as soon as the Syrian charioteers realized that the man they were pursuing was not Ahab. They drove off, looking for the missing king.

The battle is hot and heavy; while the chariots rumbled and swords are wielded, a deadly arrow, shot by a nameless archer, finds the crack in Ahab's armor:

> And a certain man drew a bow at a venture, and smote the king of Israel between the joints of the harness: wherefore he said unto the driver of his chariot, "Turn your hand, and carry me out of the host; for I am wounded." And the battle increased that day: and the king was stayed up in his chariot against the Syrians, and died at even: and the blood ran out of the wound into the midst of the chariot…And one washed the chariot in the pool of Samaria; and the dogs licked up his blood; and they washed his armour; according unto the Word of the Lord which He spoke.
> —I Kings 22:34, 35, 38

Without even *aiming*, the bowman shoots into the air and his arrow finds the only opening in the armor of the wicked king. Ahab is wounded at last by a random arrow, entering "between the scale of his armory and the breast plate" (RSV). Ahab's corpse is carried to Samaria and the dogs, following with Elijah's prophecy, lick his pooled blood (I Kings 21:19).

How could anyone doubt the fact that God has a Sovereign plan, and—come what may—it *will be accomplished*. His arrow of truth and justice will find its mark!

Justice...The Law of Love
THE FULFILLMENT OF THE WORD OF GOD

One must never forget God is all powerful as well as all seeing. He is in every place at all times: nothing can escape His knowing. By no means do the tactics of the wicked go unnoticed. God is always aware of the plots and plans of man. We are all exposed to His all-seeing eye. "And there is no creature hidden from His sight, but all things are naked and open to the eyes of Him to whom we must give account" (Hebrews 4:13).

Indeed, no man can evade God's laws with impunity. God's laws are their own executioners: there are no exemptions from punishment. Stolen waters are sweet, but every ounce of sweetness creates a pound of nausea.

Did Jezebel's judgment arrive? Absolutely—after 20 years.

Following Ahab's death, Jezebel virtually ruled the kingdom. Elijah had been taken home to heaven without the touch of the death and Elisha had succeeded him. Never forget the prophetic words sent from God will accomplish what God has promised. It might be slow in coming but change is on the way:

> And Elisha the prophet called one of the children of the prophets, and said unto him, "Gird up thy loins, and take this box of oil in your hand, and go to Ramoth-gilead: And when thou come. thither, look out there Jehu the son of Jehoshaphat the son of Nimshi, and go in, and make him arise up from among his brethren, and carry him to an inner chamber; Then take the box of oil and pour it on his head, and say, 'Thus saith the Lord, I have anointed thee king over Israel.'
>
> Then open the door and flee, and tarry not." So the young man, even the young man the prophet, went to Ramoth-gilead. And when he came, behold, the captains of the host were sitting; and he said, "I have an errand to thee, O captain." And Jehu said, "Unto which of all us?" And he said, "To thee, O captain." And he arose, and went into the house; and he poured the oil on his head, and said unto him, "Thus saith the Lord God of Israel, I have anointed thee king over the people of the Lord, even over Israel. And thou shalt smite the house of Ahab thy master, that I may avenge the blood of My servants the prophets, and the blood of all the servants of the Lord, at the hand of Jezebel…
>
> And I will make the house of Ahab like the house of Jeroboam the son of Nebat, and like the house of Baasha the son of Ahijab: And the dogs shall eat Jezebel in the portion of Jezreel, and there shall be none to bury her." And be opened the door, and fled.
>
> —II Kings 9:1–7, 9, 10

Jehu was just the man for such an occasion—furious in his anger, rapid in his movements and unscrupulous. Yet he was zealous to uphold the law of Moses:

> Then Jehu came forth to the servants of his lord: and one said unto him, "Is all well? wherefore came this mad fellow to thee?" And he said unto them, "Ye know the man, and his communication." And they said, "It is false; tell us now." And he said, "Thus and thus spake he to me, saying, 'Thus saith the Lord, I have anointed thee king over Israel.'" Then they hasted, and took every man his garment, and put it under him on the top of the stairs, and blew with trumpets, saying, "Jehu is king."
> —II Kings 9:11–13

Jehu mounted his chariot, assembled a company of his most reliable soldiers, and "furiously" drove his chariots nearly 60 miles to Jezreel:

> So Jehu rode in a chariot and went to Jezreel, for Joram was laid up there; and Ahaziah king of Judah had come down to see Joram.
>
> Now a watchman stood on the tower in Jezreel, and he saw the company of Jehu as he came, and said, "I see a company of men."
>
> And Joram said, "Get a horseman and send him to meet them, and let him say, '*Is it* peace?'"
>
> So the horseman went to meet him, and said, "Thus says the king: '*Is it* peace?'"
>
> And Jehu said, "What have you to do with peace? Turn around and follow me."
>
> So the watchman reported, saying, "The messenger went to them, but is not coming back."
>
> Then he sent out a second horseman who came to

them, and said, "Thus says the king: '*Is it* peace?'"

And Jehu answered, "What have you to do with peace? Turn around and follow me."

So the watchman reported, saying, "He went up to them and is not coming back; and the driving *is* like the driving of Jehu the son of Nimshi, for he drives furiously!"

Then Joram said,Make ready." And his chariot was made ready. Then Joram king of Israel and Ahaziah king of Judah went out, each in his chariot; and they went out to meet Jehu, and met him on the property of Naboth the Jezreelite.

Now it happened, when Joram saw Jehu, that he said, "*Is it* peace, Jehu?"

So he answered, "What peace, as long as the harlotries of your mother Jezebel and her witchcraft *are so* many?"

Then Joram turned around and fled, and said to Ahaziah, "Treachery, Ahaziah!" Now Jehu drew his bow with full strength and shot Jehoram between his arms; and the arrow came out at his heart, and he sank down in his chariot.

Then *Jehu* said to Bidkar his captain, "Pick *him* up, *and* throw him into the tract of the field of Naboth the Jezreelite; for remember, when you and I were riding together behind Ahab his father, that the Lord laid this burden upon him:

'Surely I saw yesterday the blood of Naboth and the blood of his sons,' says the Lord, 'and I will repay you in this plot,' says the Lord. Now therefore, take *and* throw him on the plot *of ground*, according to the word of the Lord."

—II Kings 9:16-26

JUSTICE...THE LAW OF LOVE

> And when Jehu was come to Jezreel, Jezebel heard of it; and she painted her face, and tired her head, and looked out at a window.
>
> —II Kings 9:30

Who is Jehu? Twenty years prior to the passage cited above, Jehu rode with Ahab to take Naboth's vineyard. And Jezebel? This same Jezebel wrote the letters condemning Naboth. And Jezreel? This is the very same place where Naboth had his vineyard and where Naboth died, his life pounded out by stones.

Consider the verse from poet Leslie Savage Clark:

From the palace casement she looked down,
Queenly, scornful, proud,
And watched with cold indifferent eyes
The weary ragged crowd.
Of the wage of sin she never thought,
Nor that a crown might fall…
Nor did she note the hungry dogs
Skulking along the wall.

As penned in the above poem, some people seem to reach a place of power and prestige, but become unaware that their feet are feet of clay—that God alone is responsible for their next breath. Many are oblivious that they are a mere heartbeat from eternity.

Note the three eunuchs in the following verse. How many times must they have seen the wicked rants of their evil queen!

> And as Jehu, the new king by the will and word of the Lord, entered in at the gate, she asked: "Had Zimri peace who slew his master?" And Jehu lifted up his face to the window and said, "Who is on my side? Who?" And there

looked out to him two or three eunuchs. And he said, "Throw her down."

—II Kings 9:3–33

These men picked up Jezebel—her tired head, painted face, bejeweled fingers and silken skirts—and threw her onto the street, her blood splattering on the streets and walls of the city, disgracing them all. Jehu drove his horses and chariot over her broken body, now crushed by the wheels.

> And when he was come in he did eat and drink, and said, "Go, see now this cursed woman, and bury her: for she is a king's daughter." And they went to bury her: but they found no more of her than the skull, and the feet, and the palms of her hands.
>
> —II Kings 9:34, 35

God Almighty *saw to it* that the hungry dogs ate the brains that conceived the plot that took Naboth's life. God Almighty *saw to it* that the mangy, back-alley dogs tore apart the hands that wrote the murderous letters. God Almighty *saw to it* that the dogs that ate carrion ravaged the feet that walked in Baal's courts—and then in Naboth's vineyard.

Jehu's soldiers returned to their leader and said, "We went to bury her, O king, but the dogs had eaten her!"

> And Jehu replied: This is the word of the Lord, which he spake by his servant Elijah the Tishbite saying, "In the portion of Jezreel shall dogs eat the flesh of Jezebel. And the carcass of Jezebel shall be as dung upon the face of the field in the portion of Jezreel; so that they shall not say, 'This is Jezebel.'"
>
> —II Kings 9:36, 37

Thus perished a female demon—the most infamous queen who ever wore a royal diadem.

Here is the justice of God: *God said it and it was done!* We can *trust* the power and certainty of God to carry out His own saving justice in providence. That all might know that His justice does not slumber! Although the judgments of God often travel slowly, they will *always* reach their desired end. The mill of God may grind slowly, but it surely grinds to powder.

When we witness Ahab falling in battle and marvel at the dogs literally eating Jezebel by the walls of Jezreel, we can agree most assuredly with Scripture,

> Oh that you had hearkened to my commandments; then had your peace been as a river, and your righteousness as the waves of the sea!
>
> —Isaiah.48:18

> As I remember how the gains of ungodliness are bought with the price of the curse of God, I must ask: Wherefore do you spend money for that which is not bread? And labour for that which satisfies not?
>
> —Isaiah 55:2

The only way for any man or woman on earth to escape the sinner's reward on earth and the torment of hell is to *make sure* you have given your life to Christ Jesus and have received the gift of eternal life.

CONCLUSION
The Way of Love
OVERCOMING BY THE BLOOD OF THE LAMB

So what is true justice?

A simplistic definition is that justice equals *fairness*. However, the justice of God involves much more than just being fair. God's court of justice is sovereign: His justice is always fair, while at the same time it can also be severe. We, God's people, need to learn to accept both of these aspects of justice from our God. On March 19, 1998, my dear prophetic friend Bob Jones received a powerful prophetic experience in which the Lord gave him Psalms 97:2:

> Clouds and thick darkness surround Him; righteousness and justice are the foundation of His throne.

The Lord *coming in clouds and thick darkness* speaks of a divine visitation bringing the justice of God and the blessings of God simultaneously. This type of visitation is a two-edged sword.

Those who have been faithful though repentance and intercession will find this season to be a season of *cleansing and blessing*. We will be cleansed and sanctified by the Spirit of Truth so we can more fully become partakers of His divine nature and His holy character. First Peter 1:4 emphasizes that we have God's precious and magnificent promises by which we become partakers of His divine nature through the true knowledge of Christ.

Those who have not been faithful to God's Word will find that this visitation will produce *judgment and divine retribution*.

The Church is being challenged to determine just how willing she will be to enter into purity and purpose. In Psalm 89:14, the truth is revealed:

> Your throne is founded on two strong pillars—the one
> is Justice and the other Righteousness. Mercy and Truth
> walk for you as your attendants. Blessed are those who
> hear the joyful blast of the trumpet, for they shall walk
> in the light of your presence.

In order for a true manifestation of the Lord's manifest presence, there must be a foundation of *righteousness and justice* in our lives and in the Church, upon which His seat of authority can be established.

Again, always rest assured that because God is for us *no one can stand against us*. Because of the plans and purposes of God for our lives, we are never the victim. On the contrary, Colossians 2:10 explains that we are *complete* in Christ, being made perfect in Love.

This completion in Christ is, in fact, the fulfillment of Justice in our lives. How is this possible? The word *complete* used in Colossians is the Greek word *plēroō*, also translated *fulfilled*. The fulfillment of *justice* in our lives is the act of *fulfilling the word of God* for our lives—and the Word of God cannot fail: "I became a minister according to the stewardship from God which was given to me for you, *to fulfill the word of God*" (Col. 1:25).

Being made complete in Christ, therefore, is to fulfill the Word of God for our lives, which enacts justice in every circumstance: Naboth was *made complete* in Love because he fulfilled the Word, offering himself as a witness for the sake of the land covenant, and justice was served on his enemies.

It was not Naboth's blood that made peace, however, nor was it Jezebel's, nor Naboth's—but the Blood of Christ, which guarantees the New Covenant between God and His people, guaranteeing our victory at every step, on every occasion. Colossians 1:20 explains that God has "reconciled all things to Himself…having made peace through the blood of His cross." It is the *Blood of Christ* which guarantees God's justice for us.

Through His Blood, we become the purchased possessions of God and are able to fulfill the plans and purposes written for us before the foundation of the world (Ephesians 1:14; 2:10).

Through His Blood, we and our family lines are brought into the Kingdom of God and cleansed from the curse of the law—because Christ became that curse for us (Galatians 3:13).

Through His Blood, His saving grace will free us from the law's cycle of sowing and reaping as we repent from our sins and walk in forgiveness.

Through His Blood, we find mercy, not judgment.

Through His Blood and the word of our testimony we become overcomers, in every situation, no matter the loss. *Because of His Blood*, nothing shall separate us from Love:

> Who shall separate us from the love of Christ? Shall tribulation, or distress, or persecution, or famine, or nakedness, or peril, or sword? As it is written: "For Your sake we are killed all day long; We are accounted

as sheep for the slaughter." Yet in all these things we are more than conquerors through Him who loved us. For I am persuaded that neither death nor life, nor angels nor principalities nor powers, nor things present nor things to come, nor height nor depth, nor any other created thing, shall be able to separate us from the love of God which is in Christ Jesus our Lord.

—Rom. 8:35–39

I pray that you may enter into the rest of God, knowing that He will *never leave you* and *never, no never, forsake you*. May we never forget that our God is a just and right God and His justice will triumph.

Bobby Conner
Eagles View Ministries
Box 1028
Moravian Falls, NC. 28654
www.bobbyconner.org